NEVADA

by Jonatha A. Brown

GARETH**STEVENS**
GS
PUBLISHING
A Member of the WRC Media Family of Companies

Please visit our web site at: www.garethstevens.com
For a free color catalog describing Gareth Stevens Publishing's
list of high-quality books and multimedia programs, call
1-800-542-2595 (USA) or 1-800-387-3178 (Canada).
Gareth Stevens Publishing's fax: (877) 542-2596.

Library of Congress Cataloging-in-Publication Data

Brown, Jonatha A.
   Nevada / Jonatha A. Brown.
      p. cm. — (Portraits of the states)
   Includes bibliographical references and index.
   ISBN-10: 0-8368-4671-0 ISBN-13: 978-0-8368-4671-3 (lib. bdg.)
   ISBN-10: 0-8368-4690-7 ISBN-13: 978-0-8368-4690-4 (softcover)
   1. Nevada—Juvenile literature. I. Title. II. Series.
   F841.3.B76   2006
   979.3—dc22   2005044479

Updated edition reprinted in 2007. First published in 2006 by
Gareth Stevens Publishing
A Weekly Reader Company
1 Reader's Digest Rd.
Pleasantville, NY 10570-7000 USA

Editorial direction: Mark J. Sachner
Project manager: Jonatha A. Brown
Editor: Catherine Gardner
Art direction and design: Tammy West
Picture research: Diane Laska-Swanke
Indexer: Walter Kronenberg
Production: Jessica Morris and Robert Kraus

Picture credits: Cover, pp. 4, 12, 15, 28 © Kerrick James.com; p. 5 © Corel;
p. 6 © Michael Ledger/Getty Images; pp. 8, 10 © Hulton Archive/Getty Images;
p. 9 © Alan Band/Getty Images; pp. 16, 18, 21, 22, 24, 25 © John Elk III; p. 17
© Nevada Historical Society; p. 26 © Jack Dykinga/Getty Images; p. 27
© Bernadette Heath; p. 29 © Matthew Stockman/Getty Images

Printed in the United States of America

2 3 4 5 6 7 8 9 10 09 08 07

CONTENTS

Words that are defined in the Glossary appear
in **bold** the first time they are used in the text.

On the Cover: Las Vegas is one of the top entertainment and tourist
centers in the United States.

Introduction

L et's take a trip to Nevada! This great state is known for wide-open spaces and high, craggy mountains. It is also known for cities full of glittering lights and all kinds of fun. Cowboys, ranches, and silver and gold mines are part of the scene, too. Nevada is a wonderful place!

You can explore dusty old ghost towns. You can ski at Lake Tahoe. You can ride jet skis and swim in Lake Mead. You can watch amazing magic and animal shows in Las Vegas. There is always something interesting to do in Nevada.

The blue waters of Lake Mead fill a desert canyon.

The state flag of Nevada.

NEVADA FACTS

- Became the 36th State: October 31, 1864
- Population (2006): 2,495,529
- Capital: Carson City
- Biggest Cities: Las Vegas, Paradise, Reno, Henderson
- Size: 109,826 square miles (284,449 square km)
- Nickname: The Silver State
- State Tree: Bristlecone pine, Single-leaf piñon
- State Flower: Sagebrush
- State Animal: Desert bighorn sheep
- State Bird: Mountain bluebird

History

Native Americans came to Nevada thousands of years ago. The people caught fish and hunted ducks for food. Some painted pictures on rocks. Some built huts of mud and sticks along rivers.

By the early 1800s, several Native tribes lived there. These people lived in peace with each other. They hunted animals and gathered wild plants for food. They built shelters out of poles and grass.

White Explorers

The first white men to reach the area were from Spain. Francisco Garcés was their leader. He may have crossed the southern part of the state in 1776. In those days,

White people forced the Native people of Nevada to move to poor, rocky land. This photo of a Native couple was taken in 1937.

First Fight

In 1833, a group of trappers traveled across Nevada. They were headed for California. Along the way, they fought with a band of Natives. It was the first battle in Nevada between Natives and whites. The Natives had never seen guns before. Many of them were killed.

nearby Mexico belonged to Spain. After breaking away from Spain, Mexico claimed the land in the early 1820s.

Traders and fur trappers began to arrive at about the same time. Most of them were from the United States and Britain. The boldest of these men blazed new trails across Nevada. Settlers later used these trails to reach California.

In the 1840s, John C. Frémont and Kit Carson explored more of this wild area. They made maps and gave names to some of the places they found. Frémont found the Carson River. He named it after Kit Carson.

War Brings Change

War broke out between Mexico and the United States in 1846. After two years of fighting, Mexico lost the war. It had to give up Nevada. Now, the area was owned by the United States. At first, this area was part of a huge **territory** that included most of the West and Southwest. Later, it became part of the Utah Territory.

Miners and Mormons

The first white settlement in Nevada was founded in 1849. This was the town of Dayton. It was settled by miners.

7

Mormons began moving to Nevada. The Mormons belonged to a church that was unpopular in some places. They raised cattle and built a trading post. Most of the other settlers in the area did not like the Mormons. Finally, in 1857, the Mormons moved to what is now Utah.

This mining camp was once a busy place. It was built in the Sierra Nevada mountains when silver ore was discovered there.

IN NEVADA'S HISTORY

A Miner's Life

Mining for silver was dangerous and hard work. Miners chipped through solid rock to make tunnels. They worked in the dark, often standing in water up to their knees. Sometimes, the roof of a tunnel caved in. A cave-in could easily kill many men.

Life was little better above the ground. The miners often lived in dirty huts or tents. The law did not mean much in their camps. These camps were not good places to raise a family.

FUN FACTS

Ghost Towns

In 1880, about 62,000 people lived in Nevada. By 1890, the number had dropped to about 47,000. Towns that had once been busy stood empty. They were known as ghost towns. Even today, visitors can still see the remains of some ghost towns in Nevada.

Famous People of Nevada

Howard Hughes

Born: Dec. 24, 1905, Houston, Texas

Died: April 5, 1976, in an airplane over southern Texas

Howard Hughes was a rich and famous man who spent some of his last years in Las Vegas. He had many claims to fame. As a young man, he was a top-notch airplane pilot. He set many flying records. Then he moved to Hollywood and produced movies. He bought movie studios and other businesses. He started his own aircraft company, too. Hughes moved to Las Vegas in 1966. While he lived there, he bought casinos, hotels, and airports. He treated his workers well and was respected for his good business sense. Hughes helped Las Vegas grow into a popular tourist spot.

In 1859, a large amount of silver was found beneath the ground near Virginia City. It was named the Comstock Lode. People rushed to Nevada, hoping to get rich. Virginia City grew to be a big mining center.

Nevada became a territory separate from Utah in 1861. Three years later, it became a U.S. state.

Problems

The new state suffered a setback in the 1870s. The

problems started when the U.S. government began to use less silver in its coins. The demand for silver fell, and some of the mines had to close. Many miners lost their jobs over the next few years. Some moved away to find work in other parts of the country.

Some people in Nevada turned to ranching. They soon found that shipping cattle by rail cost a great deal of money. This cut into the amount of money they were able to make. Then, in the late 1880s, a bitterly cold winter killed many of the cattle in the state. Some of the smaller ranchers had to sell their land.

In the late 1800s, trains like this one carried silver ore out of the mountains.

Progress

Life began to improve in the early 1900s. A big deposit of silver was found in Tonopah. Copper was found near Ely, and gold was discovered in Goldfield. Many miners came back to Nevada again.

More railroads were built, so shipping by rail became less costly. This helped the mine owners. It also helped

the ranchers. Farmers got a boost when dams were built across some of the rivers. The dammed rivers formed man-made lakes that were used for **irrigation**. Now, farmers in Nevada could water their fields and grow more crops.

The United States entered World War I in 1917. By this time, Nevada's silver and gold deposits were running low. There was still plenty of copper. It was used to make weapons during the war. When the war ended, however, there was less need for copper. Mines closed, and miners were again out of work.

The Hoover Dam

The U.S. government started to build a huge dam in 1931. It went across the Colorado River. The Hoover Dam took five years to complete. Thousands of workers were

FUN FACTS

Harold's Club

Harold's Club was the first big casino in the state. It opened in Reno in the late 1930s. People played cards and slot machines. They even bet on mice that ran around a tiny track. Harold's "rodent run" was very popular.

IN NEVADA'S HISTORY

Nuclear Testing and Nuclear Waste
In 1950, the U.S. government was looking for a place to test nuclear bombs. It chose a place near Las Vegas. Over the next forty years, hundreds of tests were done there.

Now the government wants to use Yucca Mountain as a nuclear waste dump. Many Nevadans think this plan is dangerous. They do not want nuclear waste to be stored in their state.

The Hoover Dam was built in Black Canyon on the Colorado River. Water has built up behind this huge dam to form Lake Mead.

World War II

The United States entered World War II in 1941. The mines in Nevada provided copper and lead for the war. These metals were used in guns and other supplies. Once again, miners had jobs in Nevada.

needed to build it. The dam became the biggest public works project in U.S. history. It brought many jobs to the state of Nevada.

Behind the dam, a huge lake formed. The water was used to make electric power. It was also used to irrigate crops. Three states now share the power and water provided by the dam.

Growing State

Gambling has almost always been legal in Nevada. This business began to grow in the 1930s. It is now the state's top industry. Shows, zoos, and water parks offer fun for families, too. Now, millions of **tourists** visit the state every year. Nevada is doing well, and the state is growing fast.

1776	Francisco Garcés of Spain probably travels through what is now Nevada.
1848	The United States wins the Mexican War and takes control of Nevada.
1850	The Utah Territory is formed; it includes the area that is now Nevada.
1859	The Comstock Lode is discovered; many people move to Nevada to work in the mines.
1861	The Nevada Territory is formed.
1864	Nevada becomes the thirty-sixth U.S. state on October 31.
1873	The U.S. government starts using less silver in its coins; the demand for Nevada silver starts to fall.
1900	New deposits of silver and copper are found in Nevada.
1902	A large deposit of gold is found at Goldfield.
1917–1918	The United States fights in World War I. Nevada mines provide metal for making guns and other wartime supplies.
1936	The Hoover Dam is completed.
1951	The U.S. government starts testing nuclear bombs in Nevada.
1987	Yucca Mountain is chosen to be a nuclear waste dump site.

People

Nevada is a big state with a fairly small **population**. Not quite 2.5 million people live there. Most of these people live in or near cities. Las Vegas is the largest city in the state. About six out of ten Nevadans live around this city.

Early Settlers

For thousands of years, Native Americans had the Nevada area to themselves. Few white people lived in this area until the mid-1800s. Then, the Comstock Lode

Hispanics: In the 2000 U.S. Census, 19.7 percent of the people in Nevada called themselves Latino or Hispanic. Most of them or their relatives came from places where Spanish is spoken. They may come from different racial backgrounds.

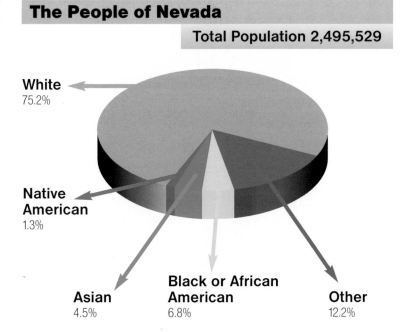

The People of Nevada

Total Population 2,495,529

White 75.2%

Native American 1.3%

Asian 4.5%

Black or African American 6.8%

Other 12.2%

Percentages are based on the 2000 Census.

Later on, settlers came to work on farms and ranches. They included families from Portugal and Italy. People from the **Pyrenees** came, too. They came to Nevada to work on sheep ranches. Many Mexicans moved to Nevada to become cowboys or field hands. Each group of people left a mark on their new home.

Nevada Today

was discovered. Thousands of whites came to work in the mines. Many of these white settlers came from the East Coast and California. Others were from Mexico. About half of the newcomers traveled to Nevada from Europe. They came from England, Scotland, Wales, and other countries.

Since the 1980s, Nevada has been the fastest growing state in the country. Most of the newcomers are from

The University of Nevada has a beautiful campus in Las Vegas. It serves thousands of students.

other parts of the United States. Mexicans are still coming to Nevada, too. In fact, more **immigrants** come from Mexico than from any other country. They bring their language and customs with them.

A small number of Native Americans still make their homes in Nevada. Many Natives live on **reservations**. African Americans, Asians, and people of mixed race live in the state, too.

Religion and Education

Nevada has more Roman

Famous People of Nevada

Sarah Winnemucca

Born: 1844, Lovelock, Nevada

Died: October 17, 1891, Monida, Montana

Sarah Winnemucca was a member of the Paiute tribe. She learned to speak English when she was young. Very few Paiutes could speak English. To help her people, she often **translated** when Paiutes and whites met to settle their differences. She also traveled to the East Coast and spoke out about the cruel ways Natives in the West were being treated. She even spoke to the U.S. Congress. Later she went back to Nevada and set up a school for Native boys and girls. The Paiutes had a special name for Sarah Winnemucca. They called her "Mother."

Catholics than people of any other faith. Many Mormons and Protestants also live there. People who practice other religions are found in smaller numbers.

Nevada has had a public school system since 1861, when it became a territory. The University of Nevada was founded in Elko four years later. It was moved to Reno in the 1880s. Today, the state has several colleges and universities. The Mackay School of Mines is one of the best known. It is also in Reno.

The Land

Nevada has three main regions. Most of the state is in the Basin and Range Region. The Sierra Nevada runs across a corner of the state near Carson City. The Columbia Plateau is in the northeast.

The Basin and Range Region

This huge region is made up of rugged mountain ranges that run from north to south. Broad valleys run between the mountain ranges. The valleys are dotted with **buttes** and **mesas**.

The highest point in the state is found in the White Mountains. It is Boundary Peak. It is 13,140 feet (4,005 meters) high. This part of the state also features many geysers and hot springs.

Little rain and snow fall in this region. Las Vegas, for example, gets only 4 inches

Great Basin National Park is a lovely place. Here, Wheeler Peak looms above the calm waters of Stella Lake.

NEVADA

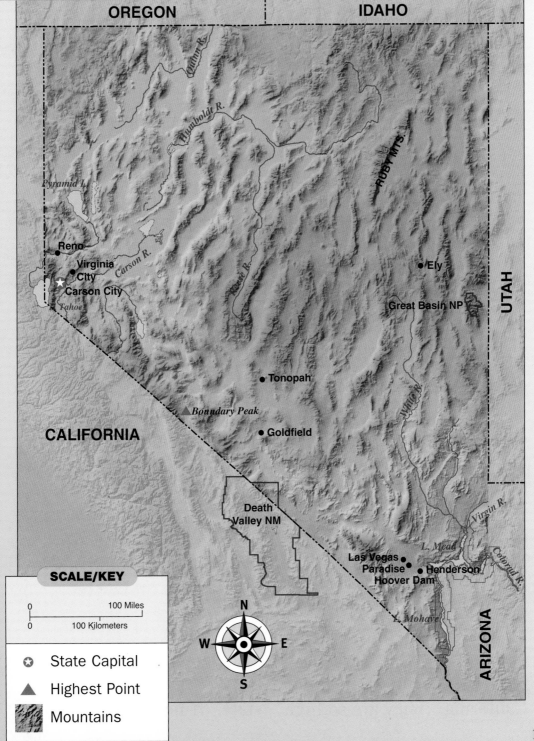

OREGON

IDAHO

Quinn R.

Humboldt R.

RUBY MTS.

Pyramid L.

Reno

Virginia
City

Carson R.

★ Carson City

Tahoe

Reese R.

UTAH

Ely

Great Basin NP

White R.

Tonopah

▲ *Boundary Peak*

CALIFORNIA

Goldfield

Death
Valley NM

Virgin R.

L. Mead

Las Vegas
Paradise
Hoover Dam

Henderson

Colorado R.

L. Mohave

ARIZONA

SCALE/KEY

0   100 Miles

0   100 Kilometers

N

W   E

S

✪ State Capital

▲ Highest Point

   Mountains

FUN FACTS

Snowy Mountains

Nevada took its name from the part of the state known as the Sierra Nevada. This area was named by Spanish explorers. Sierra means "mountain range." Nevada means "snowy." The name "Sierra Nevada" fits. The peaks are often covered with snow in the winter.

Major Rivers

Colorado River
1,450 miles (2,350 km) long

Humboldt River
290 miles (467 km)

Carson River
170 miles (275 km)

(102 millimeters) of rain a year. Cactuses and yucca grow in the desert. Coyotes, jackrabbits, tortoises, and snakes live there. Desert bighorn sheep are found in the south. Sagebrush grows further north. In the north are mule deer, foxes, and pronghorn antelope.

The Sierra Nevada

The Sierra Nevada is an area of high mountains. Most of these mountains are really in California. They are so high

that they keep rain clouds from moving east. The clouds drop most of their rain on the western side of the mountains. The eastern side is drier. In fact, Nevada is the nation's driest state. Some rain and snow do fall on the eastern side of the mountains. Single-leaf piñons grow in this region. Bristlecone pines grow there, too. They are some of the oldest trees on Earth.

The Columbia Plateau

The Columbia Plateau lies in the northeastern part of the state. It has deep valleys and high ridges. Near Idaho, canyons and cliffs give way to rolling prairies.

This part of the state has long and very cold winters. Summers are short and hot. Grasses and small, scrubby trees grow there. Mule deer, elk, and coyotes can be seen.

Waterways

Many of the riverbeds are dry most of the year. Small rivers are most likely to flow between December and June. They are the wettest months.

The Colorado River flows all year long. It forms the border between Nevada and Arizona. It is the longest river in the state.

Dams along the Colorado have created lakes. Lake

Sinks

Many rivers run into shallow spots in the ground called **sinks**. The biggest sinks are the Black Rock Desert and Smoke Creek Desert. The land there is dry most of the year. Shallow, salty lakes sometimes form in the wet season.

Mead was formed by the Hoover Dam. It is the largest lake in Nevada.

In the late 1990s, Nevada was hit by a **drought**. Lakes and rivers had much less water than usual. Heavy rains and snows in the winter of 2004-2005 helped ease the drought.

Lake Tahoe is a natural lake. It lies high in the Sierra Nevada. Tahoe is known as one of the loveliest lakes in the country.

Economy

Tourism is big business in Nevada. Millions of people visit the state each year. They go to casinos in Las Vegas and Reno. They ski at mountain resorts. They stay in hotels and eat in restaurants. All of these businesses need workers.

Products from the Land

Ranching and farming bring money to the state. Even so, these businesses are not as important as they are in some other states. About one-eighth of the land is used for farming. The leading farm product is beef

These beef cattle are grazing on a big ranch near Reno.

cattle. Sheep and dairy cattle are also important. Hay is the biggest crop. On most farms, irrigation supplies water to the fields.

Nevada produces more gold and silver than any other U.S. state. In fact, two-thirds of all the gold in the country is mined there. Oil, sand, gravel, and salt are other important products that come from the ground.

Making Goods

Most of the state's factories are in Las Vegas and Reno. Some make magazines and books. Other factories make building materials such as cement. Even candy is made in Nevada.

Henderson also has some factories. They make metal goods and chemicals. The Hoover Dam supplies power for these factories.

How Money Is Made in Nevada

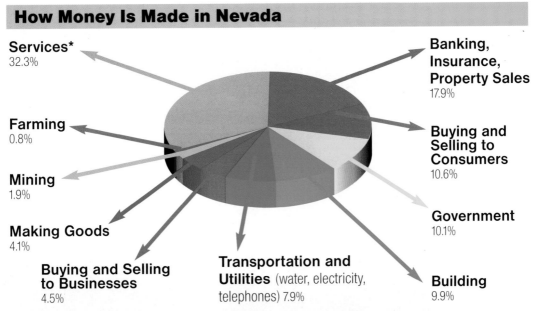

Services* 32.3%

Banking, Insurance, Property Sales 17.9%

Farming 0.8%

Buying and Selling to Consumers 10.6%

Mining 1.9%

Government 10.1%

Making Goods 4.1%

Buying and Selling to Businesses 4.5%

Transportation and Utilities (water, electricity, telephones) 7.9%

Building 9.9%

* Services include jobs in hotels, restaurants, auto repair, medicine, teaching, and entertainment.

Government

Carson City is the capital of Nevada. The leaders of the state work there. The state government has three parts. They are the executive, legislative, and judicial branches.

Executive Branch

The executive branch carries out the state's laws. The governor is the leader of this branch. More than 150 other people help the governor run this branch.

The Nevada State capitol building is in Carson City. It is famous for its large silver dome.

The Nevada State legislature meets in this large hall. The members of the legislature talk over ideas for new laws. Then they vote on whether to make the ideas into law.

Legislative Branch

The Nevada legislature has two parts. They are the Senate and the Assembly. They work together to make state laws.

Judicial Branch

Judges and courts make up the judicial branch. They may decide whether people who have been **accused of** committing crimes are guilty.

Local Government

Nevada has sixteen counties. A team of three people runs each county. Most of the cities are run by a mayor and a city council.

NEVADA'S STATE GOVERNMENT

Executive		Legislative		Judicial	
Office	Length of Term	Body	Length of Term	Court	Length of Term
Governor	4 years	Senate (21 members)	4 years	Supreme (7 justices)	6 years
Lieutenant Governor	4 years	Assembly (42 members)	2 years	District (60 judges)	6 years

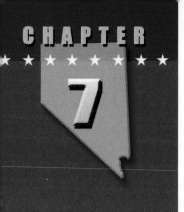

Things to See and Do

Nevada is a gorgeous state! It has so many amazing things to see. This state has deserts, forests, mountains, and lakes. Death Valley National Park is in both Nevada and California. Many people visit this park each year. They hike and bike through the desert. Great Basin National Park is farther east. It has high peaks, caves, and some of the oldest trees in the world.

State parks abound. Valley of Fire State Park has red sandstone cliffs. Visitors to the park can see pictures carved into the

This is not a scene from another planet! You can see these geysers in the Black Rock Desert.

rock by **ancient** peoples. Cathedral Gorge State Park has high cliffs carved by wind and water. Other parks feature hot springs, geysers, wetlands, and caves.

The Hoover Dam

Each year, millions of people visit the Hoover Dam. Some take a tour into the dam itself. They ride an elevator down to the bottom of the dam. Visitors also spend time at Lake Mead, the huge lake created by the dam. There they can camp, fish, swim, and enjoy other water sports.

Museums and More

Reno and Las Vegas are great places to learn about history in Nevada. Museums in

Fun Underground!

Carson City is home to the Nevada State Museum. The museum has wildlife displays and a great coin collection. It also has very realistic mining exhibits. They are housed in tunnels under the ground. Visitors go into the tunnels. There, they can see how miners worked long ago.

Valley of Fire State Park is in the Mohave Desert. The view from White Dome Road is amazing.

Famous People of Nevada

Frank Sinatra

Born: December 12, 1915, Hoboken, New Jersey

Died: May 14, 1998, Los Angeles, California

Frank Sinatra always wanted to be an entertainer. His first hit record, "All or Nothing at All," came out in 1943. It made him a big star. Many say he was the first superstar ever. Certainly, he was one of the most famous singers of his day. He starred in several movies, too. For many years, Sinatra lived in Las Vegas. His shows were popular, and he often sang to packed houses.

both cities display Native baskets, old cattle brands, and much more

Both Las Vegas and Reno have good zoos. Yet zoos are not the only places to see live animals. Animal shows are common in both cities. These shows star dolphins, horses, and other creatures that perform tricks. These shows are fun for both children and adults.

Sports

In Nevada, college sports draw thousands of fans. The University of Nevada

The bright lights of Reno have been attracting tourists for many years.

Famous People of Nevada

Andre Agassi

Born: April 29, 1970, Las Vegas, Nevada

Andre Agassi is a famous tennis player. He was named the top U.S. player when he was only eighteen years old. Now, he is one of the few players who have won all four events in the Grand Slam of tennis. Andre is not the only famous athlete in his family. His father was a famous boxer in Iran. Both father and son have competed in the Olympic Games.

has strong basketball and football teams. Their games are always well attended.

Golf is a popular sport, too. Nevada has more than one hundred golf courses. In the fall of each year, the Las Vegas Invitational Golf Tournament is held. This event draws top players from all over the world.

In the winter, skiers head to Squaw Valley and Lake Tahoe. These resort areas have outstanding slopes and good snow cover. When the weather is warmer, rodeos draw big crowds. The U.S. Team Roping Championship is in Winnemucca. Teams show off their roping skills and compete for prizes.

accused of — blamed for

ancient — very, very old

buttes — flat-topped hills with steep sides

casino — a place where people can bet money while they play different kinds of games

drought — a long period with very little rain or snow

immigrants — people who leave one country to live in another country

irrigation — a system of canals and pipes that carry water from a river or stream to farmers' fields

mesas — mountains or hills with flat tops and steeply sloping sides

population — the total number of people who live in a place, such as a state

Pyrenees — a chain of mountains that runs between France and Spain

reservations — land set aside by the government for a special use, such as land set aside for use by a group of Native Americans

sinks — large, low spots in the ground where water collects

territory — land that belongs to a country but is not yet a state

tourists — people who travel for pleasure

translated — explained what someone said in another language

Books

Death Valley National Park. True Books (series). David Petersen (Children's Press)

Nevada. United States (series). Paul Joseph (Abdo & Daughters)

Nevada Facts and Symbols. The States and Their Symbols (series). Karen Bush Gibson (Bridgestone Books)

S Is for Silver: A Nevada Alphabet. Discover America State By State (series). Eleanor Coerr (Sleeping Bear Press)

Sierra. Diane Siebert (HarperCollins)

Web Sites

Enchanted Learning: Kit Carson: American Explorer
www.enchantedlearning.com/explorers/page/c/carson.shtml

Enchanted Learning: Nevada
www.enchantedlearning.com/usa/states/nevada/index.shtml

Nevada Kids Page
dmla.clan.lib.nv.us/docs/kids/fun.htm

Portraits of Nevada
www.unr.edu/sb204/theatre/

Sierra Safari Zoo
www.sierrasafarizoo.org

INDEX